Potty Training

Revolutionized

Potty Learning Sure-Fire Natural Strategies

to Nurture Babies, Toddlers and Kids

Developing Mind

Kathleen Patel

ISBN: 978-1-63750-227-3

Table of Contents

Introduction

In this pioneering, practical book, parenting expert Kathleen Patel offer a revolutionary approach to child parenting with key strategies that foster healthy brain development, leading to calmer, happier children successful with potty learning. I explain—and make accessible—the new science of how a child's brain is wired and how it matures enough to handle potty activity efficiently and independently. The "upstairs brain," which makes decisions and balances emotions, and in young children, the right brain and its emotions tend to rule over the logic of the left brain, which is why effective potty training strategy is required for effective potty learning. By applying these ultimate strategies and discoveries to everyday parenting, you can turn any outburst, argument, or fear into a chance to integrate your child's brain and foster vital growth.

With age-appropriate strategies for dealing with day-to-day potty struggles and illustrations that will help you explain and teach these concepts to your child, This book shows you how to cultivate healthy emotional and intellectual development skills for potty training so that your children can lead balanced, meaningful, and connected lives independently.

"[A] useful potty training with child-friendly approach for loving parents. . . "— Rick Reviews

"Strategies for getting a toddler to be successful [with] potty learning."—The Washington Post

"It's an erudite, resourceful, and potty book filled with

fresh ideas based on the latest toilet/potty training research. I urge all parents who want kind, happy, and emotionally healthy kids to read this book. it is my new baby gift."—Louise Carmeer, Ph.D., Lover of "Pampers Sensitive Water-Based Baby Diaper Wipes"---

"Gives parents and teachers ideas to get all parts of a healthy child's brain working together."—Parent to Parent.

Let's Talk Potty

Do you actually spend one full day on extreme non-formal lessons or teaching for your kids and then expect your son or daughter to pass the test by the end of the day? Would you demand that he or she show mastery every day thereafter without ever making any errors?

I question it! If you do approach lessons in this manner, you'd likely finish up frustrated as well as your child would maintain tears.

The actual way that people teach children new skills is by carrying it out gradually, over an interval of days, weeks, celebrating every little victory that follows. This won't apply merely to toddlers, it's a design you'll follow as an adult for quite some time too, which include your son or daughter; from the first new experience on riding bicycle, to the very first time on skis, to the new level of driving a car, and in regards to a million other new things we all do.

Considering your part in your son or daughter's learning processes, how will you strategies when teaching your son or daughter something new?

Are you going to be extreme and psychological?

Would you demand that he sit down still and give

consideration?

Would you put a crayon in his hands and demand that he starts painting, when you sit down and get worried that he'll never figure out how to draw an effective picture or print a capital A?

Would you consider yourself seated next to him, taking records, when he would get to a better level?

Would you fret that he'll be putting on Velcro sneakers to senior high school or you need to button his tux for him on his big day?

Obviously not! You understand that your son or daughter will get good at these skills and many more during his or her lifetime which teaching him or her is one of your jobs as a mother or father.

Think about your expectations when teaching your son or daughter something new. When teaching him to draw an image of the family, what do you anticipate to be the very first thing he'll deposit on paper? A family group portrait? No, it's a scribble! And you will take pleasure in his work and post his artwork on the refrigerator door. As time passes, and with repetition, that scribble will need shape till your son or daughter will pull circles and squares and soon homes, people, and pets.

Now let look at this next new event in your son or daughter's life: *Potty/Toilet training.* You should be able to strategize potty training the same manner that you do every other new skills step-by-step, as time passes, with pleasure, kindness, and endurance. Let discuss those important strategies needed to ensure a smooth potty training.

At the beginning of the grand experience of teaching a child to use the potty, many parents question how they'll ever accomplish such a complex task. They watch their toddler with his brand-new potty dish on his head playing and questioning the sanity that persuaded them as a parent to buy the potty initially. The glad tidings are that almost all children have the ability to get better at daytime toilet/potty training at age three (3) to five (5) roughly, and for some families it's a nice, even fun experience.

CHAPTER 1

What You Should Know about Potty Training

When to Start

You can start potty training a kid at any age: you can even set a new baby on the potty bowl. However, *the most crucial question is; when will the training be finished?* A kid will complete potty/toilet training when his biology, skills, and development have matured to a spot that he's able and willing to dominate complete control of his toileting. Only then can he or she recognizes the necessity to stop his or her game, go directly to the toilet, handle the whole process, and go back to his or her game.

The quantity of time it requires for your son or daughter

to understand toilet training is closely related to the span between your commencement of the training and the strategies applied; few months old when you begin training and when he or she is physically and emotionally in a position to take responsibility. Several studies also show that no matter when the potty or toilet training starts, nearly all children are just physically endowed with the capacity of 3rd party toileting after age group two, and mastery usually happens between age range two (2) and four (4).

Keeping Things Ready

Not only will it be that you don't need to hurry the procedure, simply because rushing things can result into disaster. It places incredible stress on both you and your child. It makes the complete process a miserable experience rather than the normal learning process that it ought to be. A lot more, when stress and pressure enter the picture, it can create tantrums, constipation, extreme mishaps, and setbacks.

Your son or daughter will figure out how to use the toilet. She'll learn best in her own way and on her behalf own time plan. There is absolutely no award for the most quickly trained child. And research proves again that early or past due toileting mastery has nothing at all whatsoever regarding how smart or intelligent a kid is. So relax and revel in the process.

Can You Start Before Readiness?

A kid can be placed on the toilet bowl even while still a child, and in a few cultures this is routinely done. A little percentage of American and Canadian parents have followed this practice, called EC. Before you subscribe to thinking your daily life just got a lot easier, you should know that EC is not toilet training. It really is a long-lasting, soft, gradual system that can be used rather than diapers to control a child's waste materials. It replaces hourly diaper changes with hourly trips to the toilet.

With this technique, parents read their baby's body language and sound cues to put her on the toilet container when they believe that it is time on her behalf to defecate. The mother or father manages the child's defecation process before child is literally mature with the capacity of total individual toileting which often happens at the age range mentioned previously: from two to four years old.

If the thought of changing diapers with the strategy of watching your son or daughter's body signals and putting him or her on the potty suits you, then research one of the numerous books on this issue known as infant toilet training. In this toilet training book, we'll strategize toilet training from the more prevalent toddler-readiness approach.

Can You Get it Done in a Day?

For the vast majority of families who consider toilet training a toddler event, some can look for a fast-fix solution. However, even those interesting books or programs that guarantee one-day results have a significant stipulation: they recommend using the ideas only once a kid shows all the symptoms of readiness and reaches a starting age group of about 2yrs. In addition, they warn that bad incidents might occur for weeks afterward and the mother or father must be diligent to keep taking the kid to the toilet on a regular basis.

Can You Get it Done in a Day?

For many families who consider toilet training a toddler event, some can look for a fast-fix solution. However, even those interesting books or programs that guarantee one-day results have a significant stipulation: they recommend using the ideas only once a kid shows all the symptoms of readiness and reaches a starting age group of about 2yrs. In addition, they warn that bad incidents might occur for weeks afterward and the mother or father must be diligent to keep taking the kid to the toilet on a regular basis.

How Long Does it Take a Child to Learn?

When toilet/potty training starts at about age group two,

it can take from three (3) months to a year of toilet training before the child gains potty independence. Generally, the younger the kid is, the fewer readiness skill she possesses; the greater a mother or father must be engaged, and the much longer chance of success would take.

Regardless of your method of toilet training, 98% of children are completely independent by age four. (Nighttime dryness is another issue, predicated on physiology, and may take a lot longer.)

Can Potty Training be Considered a Child-Led Decision?

When deciding when to begin potty training, you will certainly want to think about your child's readiness and interest. However, if you wait around until that magic day whenever your child approaches you with a formal demand to begin potty training, you might be waiting for a very long time. A kid simply doesn't understand the worthiness of moving out of diapers to toilet independence. A kid doesn't have the knowledge, wisdom, references, or intelligence to make this kind of decision by him or herself.

Let's consider these;

Do you let your son or daughter decide his own bedtime? Do you let him take the on business lead when he'll dress himself? Do you want to allow him to choose when he's prepared to begin kindergarten?

Your son or daughter counts on you to make many decisions for him or her. Despite the fact that he'd prefer to go to sleep at 10 p.m., you will decide whenever he's exhausted and yawning at 7 p.m. that is clearly a much better choice. And while he or she may want to get on the school bus along with his old brother, you understand that he's nowhere near ready for school.

Among your important assignments as a mother or father is to make decisions for your son or daughter until he or she actually is ready to make some of these trivial decisions on his or her own. With regards to potty or toilet training, she needs you to observe her for readiness cues and sunsequently apply this book ideas and strategies to her when you are feeling she's prepared to accept it and be potty trained. And you also are very experienced to get this done, because you almost certainly know your son or daughter much better than she understands herself.

Parenting Factor for Potty Decisions

Toilet/potty training isn't just an all or nothing decision. Many parents start the procedure early with the youngster because they might instead assist, remind, and tidy up a few mishaps than continue steadily to change diapers. Some decide to begin by slowly watching their child's body signals to advance to each new level. Others concentrate intently on strategies with expectations to make things work swiftly.

Any path you select for your baby can work, as long as you are positive and patient. Regardless of your plan, it can help to go from diapers to total self-reliance. For most parents, halfway is not a bad spot to be, even if indeed they spend half a year at that midpoint.

Parenting is filled up with choices, and the ultimate decisions are incredibly different for each family. There is not just one single right to toilet train or potty train a child; the methods are extensive. The right strategy for you is the one that feels convenient to you and works for you as well as your child. Eventually, you will have to assess what your loved one's goals are and then arranged an idea that is most effective for you.

Potty Training and Potty Learning

The conditions *potty training* and *toilet training* have been around for decades and will be the conditions that a lot of people use to spell out the procedure. However, it isn't really about training at all, it is approximately **teaching and learning**. So; a far more accurate label for the procedure would be toilet learning or toilet teaching. With this thought, I polled more than 250 (two hundred and fifty) parents about their selection of conditions. While most of them decided it is actually about learning,

95% were sensed to be convenient with the traditional methodology and said that if indeed they were searching for a reserve on this issue, they might search the normal phrases. So throughout this reserve, I'll stick to the time honored conditions of toilet training and potty training but as you and I both know, it's a teaching/learning process.

Basic Essentials for Potty Training a Child

There can be an enormous market for potty training paraphernalia, such as expensive dolls that soak and wet, specially made toilet chair, tot-sized urinals, fancy charts, posters, prizes, and awards. While many of these can easily make for a great experience, it isn't in any way necessary to buy a range of products for such a very simple, natural process.

A potty chair, twelve pairs of training jeans, and a relaxed and enjoyable ambiance of learning are what's needful to teach your son or daughter how to use the toilet or potty. Anything extra is optional.

Helpful Facts about Potty Training

You probably don't believe much about your potty process, and it's probably so because the color and uniformity of your son or daughter's diaper deposits have been part of your daily activities. There are a few facts that are beneficial to know as you attempt the potty/toilet training journey.

- Potty training has nothing in connection with nighttime dryness. Nighttime dryness is achieved only once a child's physiology facilitates it. A kid bed-wets while asleep due to some amount of reasons: his kidneys aren't sending a sign to his brain when he's asleep to alert him he must go pee or poo, his bladder hasn't yet grown large enough to accommodate urine all night, his bladder overproduces urine at night time, or he sleeps so deeply that he doesn't stay awake to visit the toilet. As children develop, many of these conditions are personally corrected. This usually occurs between the age range of three (3) and six (6). This is not something you can educate, and you can't rush it.

- *A parent's readiness to teach is as crucial as a child's readiness to learn.* A kid can't understand how to use the toilet unless someone shows him or her. As well as the teacher's strategy and attitude can have a direct impact on how long the procedure takes and exactly how pleasurable the journey would be. A parent who is stressed about the process or who's too busy to dedicate enough time necessary for teaching can gradually complicate the procedure, or even take it to a screeching halt. Conversely, an educated, patient mother or father with a pleasurable strategy can make the process pleasurable and bring far better, and quicker result.

- Most toddlers urinate four to eight times every day, usually about every two hours roughly. A child's bladder can hold one and a half ounces of urine for every year old. (A two-year-old's bladder can take about 2-3 ounces; a three-year-old's, around 3 to 4.5 ounces; and a four-year-old's, about 4-6 ounces-less when compared to a cup.)

- Most toddlers have a couple of bowel patterns every day; some have three, while others neglect a day or two among patterns. Generally, each young one has a regular pattern.

- A child's diet will influence the total amount and frequency of urination and bowel motions. Adequate daily liquids, including drinking water, plus a nutritious diet comprising foods with a lot of fiber (fruits, vegetables, and wholegrain) can make reduction easier, which subsequently makes toilet training more comfortable.

- Ample daily exercise means that your son or daughter's stool is shifted through her system correctly. Insufficient movement can lead to constipation.

- A child's pelvic and sphincter muscles need to relax to be able to release a pee or poop. Stress, pressure, or panic is a surefire way to avoid the procedure. (That is why some children use their diaper soon after they are coming out of the toilet.).

- Polls show that more than 80 percent of parent say that their children experience some set back in toilet training. This high number indicates that what we often label as "setbacks" is just the most common way to mastery of toileting. Exactly like any new thing that children learn, it isn't always a smooth process from beginning to end. It's similar to a squiggly range, with bursts of success as well as nags and pauses on the way to the ultimate result.

- It doesn't seem to really matter what strategy can

be used for toilet teaching/potty training, because 98% of children are entirely time-independent at age group four (4).

CHAPTER 2

Importance of Elimination Communication

Elimination Communication is the practice that involves making use of your child's cues to greatly help them get rid of their waste. For some, it appears like zero diaper use ever, while for others, it's a mixture of using diapers. It doesn't actually matter how long you've used EC or how regular.

Now, you're scanning this, which means no matter current EC literature, you understand in your heart, it's sure for completion. I'm likely to call this completion procedure a "bridge," for brevity; a bridge from there to here.

I actually contacted some EC specialists because increasingly more people wish to potty train before twenty weeks. I completely support this but discovered this might be a particular percentage of Elimination Communication and a specific percentage of Potty training.

However, below are several things that are part of EC that may make potty training a little difficult.

1. Diaper-free Time.

2. Getting the pee, not shifting to the potty.

3. Philosophy.

4. The idea that your son or daughter will simply potty train themselves.

5. The expectation that EC offers you a joint potty training.

6. Potty strike.

Diaper-free Time

We don't know about your position but also for many parents, Diaper-free Period gets misconstrued. For most, Diaper-free time probably condition your son or daughter to pee on to the floor.

I've heard many tales of children who just stay naked all day long with parents attempting catches but really just clearing up a whole lot of pee. I talked to numerous EC experts over time. I couldn't wrap my head for this particular practice.

There's just therefore much to learn that every moment can be an experiment and discovery. So if they pour their milk away on the ground, it's for the pleasure of viewing, "Oh . . . this occurs when I do that. Great."

Nevertheless, it's our work as parents to tell them that pouring milk on the floor isn't suitable. While we wouldn't yell or shame them, we'd consistently most likely frown and say something comparable to, "No, no . . . zero milk stays up for grabs."

So, now let's consider the cause and after-effect of peeing anywhere, anytime the desire hits. If you never let your kid know that it's unacceptable, you won't like the aftermath effect. It's consequently learned behavior to simply pee where you have to pee. This may be okay in the first days, whatever age group you started elimination communication, but once your child regularly does this for just about any big chunk of period, it's kind of cemented in. In other terms, you've traded a diaper for your floor.

The only reason I talk about Diaper-free Time is since the initial thing I hear from an EC Mama is level of resistance to a naked day time.

The naked day time is quite crucial to one of the largest steps in building the bridge from EC to PT, which lead us to issue number 2.

Getting Pee, and not on a Potty

So far in EC, you almost certainly have an incredible bond with your child. You understand her signals and you hurry to take her potty, mostly where it's convenient. I really like the actual fact that EC offers you "permission" to potty anywhere. Nevertheless, once you officially begin potty schooling, you do need to get your son or daughter to the potty of choice (either the tiny potty or the place on the toilet). The big thing here's getting the child physically to the correct place. However, the norm is to be getting the kid to the potty. I'd say this task alone may be the biggest in the bridge from there to here.

Philosophy

I understand that "traditional potty schooling" is a dirty

term in EC. I understand there are "shoe camps" for potty training and all types of coercive methods or advice. However, at times I discover myself having to remind parents that it's alright to possess boundaries and objectives. There's a whole lot of philosophy around

EC and attaching parenting that sometimes falls aside as your son or daughter nears the twos. I don't think the twos have to be terrible by any stretch, nevertheless, you may find that a few of this EC-associated philosophy doesn't endure. I don't wish to argue this aspect, and I'm not really saying anything about anyone's parenting design. I just find this as certainly a difficult place in parenting to keep up theory. Your child will begin limit screening, and his favourite word is going to be "No."

Most of the philosophy suggests that there may be nothing bad around the potty.

Very much as in the "milk on to the floor" cause-and-effect example, you do need to tell your son or daughter what your positive expectation is and what the adverse expectation is. This doesn't have to sound mean, but you do have to mean business. At some time your child must find out that peeing simply anywhere is a "don't." A lot of parents emphasize the positive end of issues ("just pee in the potty"), but they omit the other section of the equation ("don't pee somewhere else"). Therefore, yes, you definitely want to emphasize the positive, but be sure you are getting clear in what you don't need as well.

Expecting Your Toddler to Potty Teach Him or Herself

Occasionally a child will opt to potty himself. Generally, this is simply not the case, however, which makes feeling if you think about any of it. And that's most likely why you are right here. Peeing and pooping are primal behaviors, do you agree? You don't need to teach a child how exactly to pee or poop. Placing it in a container of some kind is a socialized behavior. Socialized behavior should be taught, the simplest way to obtain it is to slap it all out of your hands. That's primal. The socialized way of setting it up is to ask or negotiate. That's what should be taught.

How do we train that?

When our kids utilize the primal instinct to slap something out of someone's hand, we gaze at them in the eye, we say in a fairly stern voice, "Zero hitting. You ask." We most likely frown or make a disapproving facial expression. We are far better whenever we use simple vocabulary. "No this, Yes that." There doesn't have to be a ton of discussion about this. I think most of us, as a whole are doing a significant amount of talking. I specifically think that is true in potty teaching. It's similar to your son or daughter learning the ABCs. They aren't learning all of the power behind the letters that produce different sounds at differing times in an incredible number of combinations. In potty training, the brief, more direct words function best.

The Expectation That Elimination Communication Offers You Potty Training

I believe bridging EC with PT is the hardest part with respect to coping with the expectation that because you've been functioning at this for a reasonably long time, this will become easy for your son or daughter. Trust me, I think this will be true as well. I don't desire you to end up being mad at me, but I've discovered that this isn't necessarily the case. It's a genuine freaking bummer.

And the actual fact that you're most likely not to get one is actually hard to wrap your mind around. What I've found is that once you're more than the hump, ECed children tend to move considerably faster and the training "sticks" far better. And you possess the bonus of not just a great relationship but also of understanding your child's signals.

What I've found is most effective for ECers who wish to potty teach is to simply consider this as another (separate) process. Your son or daughter most likely hasn't made the bond that she is normally the main one who should be in action after the feeling of experiencing to pee strikes. As well as your child is probably extremely used to peeing as the urge hits. It's the slightest adjustment which will make this much easier. Another pitfall is whenever your child is definitely taking longer than typical.

CHAPTER 3

Pre-Potty Training

When kids learn a new skill, they rarely learn it all at one time. Typically, they process the information in manageable pieces. You have to believe and understand how your son or daughter learn to process and respond to information. The process began in the past when he was a child and learned to carry up his mind and shoulders and also to control his body. He progressed to sitting down, after that to crawling, and to walking while you hold him by hand. Shortly he was cruising the home furniture. After a period, he took those initial shaky steps, as soon as those were perfected, he began to walk. This organic sequence of occasions took from ten to twenty weeks.

Just as that you patiently and methodically helped your

son or daughter learn to do things naturally, you can motivate him to understand the countless details involved in potty training before you actively start potty training, that can do a lot of things that set your son or daughter up for catching up with the learning process when it's high time.

Identify the Act

Each time you change your son or daughter's diaper, you have an opportunity to train a bit about elimination. Making casual comments about elimination is an excellent method to teach. Take for instance, *"You have poopoo in your diaper."* Or, *"Your diaper is wet because you peed. Mommy pees in the potty."*

A few brief explanations as time passes are helpful. You can clarify that the wetness is pee-pee and the dark brown stuff is poopoo. Inform him or her that they are leftovers that her body doesn't need. Explain a clean, dried out diaper is a lot nicer to wear.

Help your child recognize what's taking place when you see that she's wetting or filling her diaper:

Luckily for you, if you capture her tinkling in the toilet bowl or if you feel that unexpected warmth in her diaper while carrying her. At this period you can explain what she's carrying out and let her understand that in a period like that she'll learn to perform it in the potty.

Teaching the Vocabulary

Throughout your everyday events, coach your toddler, the phrases and meanings of toilet-related terminologies such as body parts, urination, bowel motions, and toilet duties. When enough time comes for real potty schooling, there is so very much to learn, so that it will be useful if he or she currently is more comfortable with the necessary information.

Lots of terms that are used during potty training aren't directly toilet-related but can make different concepts for your son or daughter to comprehend. Descriptive words that you'll use during the procedure are those like wet, dry, clean, flush, and toilet paper (tissue paper).

Teach your child the idea of opposites and specific purposes which will give a foundation for toilet training. Wet/dried out, on/off, messy/clean, up/down, stop/proceed, now/later, these are concepts that'll be part of the potty training routine.

It's common for parents to employ a mixture of phrases and terms during the potty process, but doing this can confuse a fresh trainee. If for instance, you question him if he would "go potty," however, the next day you asked him "to go use the toilet," and later consult him if he must "tinkle," he might not follow your school of thought. It is best if you choose your vocabulary conditions and adhere to them during the training process.

Keep the Training Natural

Babies and also toddlers accept things that happen in their diaper as normal and natural. It is not until siblings, peers, and adults instruct them there's some factor disgusting about these procedures that they think in another case. Try to let your son or daughter maintain this innocent view-point about elimination. This can help toilet teaching, and potty training becomes a more definite knowledge without any embarrassment or shame. Don't attach negative worth to wet or messy diapers.

(Ensure you avoid words like miserable, icky, stinky or smelly) Do not make a significant creation about the smell or consistency, and do your very best to caution your son or daughter's big brothers and sisters about this!

The Worthiness of Demonstrations

It can be beneficial to let your child see you or her siblings utilize the toilet. You won't need to have her view every detail; it's much enough to have her discover you take a seat on the toilet bowl while you explain what you are doing. Tell her that whenever she gets heavily pressed, she'll place her pee-pee and poo-poo in the toilet, too, rather than in her diaper.

If your son or daughter has older siblings, cousins, or friends, tell her that they used diapers when they were her age, however now they utilize the toilet. If they're available to accompany in the toilet, let your baby get a glimpse of his or her sibling or peer using the potty. Allow her understand that when she gets just a little older, she'll produce that act, too.

Don't assume all parent is ready to have little eye viewing while they utilize the toilet, and it's not essential for you to do that. If you like your privacy, after that teach your son or daughter to respect a shut bathroom and toilet door. Remember that as your son or daughter masters her very own toileting, she is more likely to stick to in your footsteps and desire her personal privacy as well. Set up the toilet so that it's safe and sound and manageable on her behalf, and keep hearing open when she actually is alone in the toilet.

Carefully Select Your Potty Words!

Certain words are normal in particular geographic areas, plus some are more trusted than others. If you pay attention to daycare, the recreation center, or the retail shopping center, you'll soon know very well what words are normally used in town.

Here are a few of the words most used by families with small children:

Body Terms: Urination, bowel movement, vulva (everything you can see) and vagina (the canal inside), penis, buttocks/rectum, flatulence.

Family Words: Toilet, pot, potty, privy, loo pee, pee-pee, move potty, go pee-pee, tinkle, pissy, wee-wee, go wee, wee, wees, tee-tee, visit the bathroom, visit the toilet, utilize the potty, go (as in, "will you go?") poop, poopie, poo-poo, poos, caca, BM, move poo-poo, number two, utilize the potty, vulva, vagina, privates, bottom level, girl parts, penis, willy bottom level, bum, tush, toches/tucks, cheeks, fanny, behind, buns, rear gas, passing gas, passing wind, fart*, toot, breaking wind, blow off, poot, fluffer, stinker, etc. are regarded a rude term for children in a few families but regular in others.

Certain scientific or specialized terminologies sound odd when used with a kid. Can you envisage yourself asking your baby, "Have you got pressure in your rectum indicating that you need to defecate?" Instead, choose words that you'd be comfortable having your son or daughter use and understand fast. Use whatever phrases with which your loved ones is preferred and familiar; remember that these words will likely be called or used by your child in a general public place, so it is safer to adhere to socially acceptable language.

Promote Your Son or Daughter's Independence

This is the time to encourage your son or daughter to do things on her behalf, for example; putting on her socks, draw up her pants, remove her jacket, carry a plate to the desk, and climb directly into her car seat. All of these tasks nurture a sense of independence, which will be essential for potty mastery.

As your son or daughter masters each task, her degree of confidence will develop. The more she can perform, the more she'll be ready to try. Each achievement builds on previous successes, as well as your child will discover herself to be someone who can try brand new things and be proficient at performing them. This attitude will become especially helpful when it's to introduce potty training.

When Should You Buy a Potty Seat?

Some parents prefer to wait to buy a potty chair until active training begins, since the appearance of a brand fresh object usually causes a spike in interest. Others prefer to get a potty and place it in the toilet a few months in advance to get their child familiar with it. If you elect to obtain a potty seat before schooling begins, you might want to present it to your son or daughter with an enthusiastic tone of voice and allow her take a seat on it. Allow her to consider the pieces aside and open up and shut the lid, if it offers one.

When you get this fresh item home, speak to your child on its purpose. You can also invite your son or daughter to take a seat on her potty by using the big toilet. You can keep it in the toilet for a couple weeks or even more to let your son or daughter get utilized to the idea prior to the teaching process commencement.

If you opt to wait until teaching commences, ensure that you choose the potty and take it out from the box and place it jointly before presenting it to your son or daughter.

Importance of Reading to Your Todller

Most kids enjoy books and like to be read to. Many great children's books, created precisely for toddlers, can be found on potty training. Make an effort to get those books which have photographs of kids with books that make use of colorful pictures of pets and likely creatures learning how exactly to use the toilet.

Reading these books before training can help your son or

daughter become familiar with the theory in a fun, non-threatening way without expectations attached. You can even make use of these same books as potty-time reading when teaching begins.

Understanding How to Follow Instructions

When you begin active potty training, your child would want to know how exactly to adhere to your instructions. "Enter into the toilet." "Pull down your slacks." "Take a seat on the potty." The set of instructions will end up being long.

Start now giving your son or daughter simple directions and supporting him follow them. Request him to place a toy in the toy package. Ask her to place the glass in the sink.

At first you will have to do a large amount of prompting

and reminding. You may have to move with her to greatly help her perform your request. As time passes, she'll begin to accomplish things on her very own. When she does, praise her and encourage her with hugs and kisses. Let her understand you're pleased with her being a wonderful girl.

Helping your child to understand and stick to directions are important steps essential for successful toilet and potty training.

Chapter 4

How to Read a Child's Body Signals for Potty Activities

Understanding your child's body signal for potty activities enable you to help him or her get to the toilet fast.

The following are some typically common signals of an imminent bowel movement:

- Timing (very first thing each morning or ten to thirty minutes after a meal).

- Passing-by repeatedly.

- Squatting.

- Touching diaper.

- Tensed facial expression.

- Grunting.

- Stopping active play.

- Bending forward while holding tummy.

- Stomach-ache.

And below are a few common signals of impending urination:

- Timing (very first thing on awakening each morning or after a nap, one and half hour (1.5hrs) to two hours (2hrs) after last pee, or twenty (20) to forty-five minutes (45mins) after drinking).

- Holding crotch.

- Sitting on heels.

- Crossing legs.

- Squeezing thighs together.

- Squirming and wiggling (the potty dance).

- Bouncing.

- Shifting from feet to foot.

- Rocking backward and forwards.

- Becoming still and motionless.

- Whimpering.

The most crucial thing to bear in mind is that it is their (kids) accomplishment and milestone, not yours as a parent. ***It is important to be sensitive to their timeline.***

The more we support them in having their success and their very own accomplishment (with only a small amount of psychological attachment on our side), the quicker the achievement and the more pleasant the knowledge for kids and parents!

When your child's day to day routine is disrupted or when he's overtired, hungry, or overstimulated, he'll likely have significantly more accidents and become more forgetful in what he or she is said to be doing.

Teaching your kid how to utilize the toilet is unarguably a permanent lesson. Between dried outruns and real potty calls, you will probably find yourself accompanying him to the toilet up to a dozen times a day! That results in 84 times support to the toilet over a week and some 360 times per month!

One method to keep perspective is to write down the starting day of potty teaching and note another time of about 90 days to the future. Understand that you'll end up being your kid's potty partner for at least those 90 days. Remember, it could take typically three (3) to a year of schooling until your son or daughter will be ultimately toilet independence depending on the pace of learning and teaching strategies applied by you.

CHAPTER 5

Potty Training Your Child

Having decided that the time is here to commence potty and toilet training, your son or daughter is ready and you're prepared. So, what's next?

Firstly, ensure that your attitude and expectations are in the best place. You ought to be feeling calm and positive. It's also advisable to understand that the training process may take as long as half a year or more, so forget about any hope you may have to toilet train your toddler in merely a day. Exactly like learning how to walk, chat, or take beverage from a cup, understanding how to utilize the toilet bowl, and really should end up being a gradual, pleasurable experience for you both.

Before you place a potty in the toilet, it is time to create your supplies and execute a little planning. Below are the necessary measures to take.

Choosing Your Potty-Training Approach

There isn't just one single best way to potty train a child.

There are various approaches that can lead you to success. As you make decisions about how exactly to begin this grand endeavor, have a few things to consider:

- What is your son or daughter's learning design? How has he or she learned various other new skills? Will he or she observe and absorb before she tackles something? Or will he or she dive in and function her method through it? Is he or she a thoughtful listener or a hands-on doer?

- What exactly do you do that mostly motivates him or her to try something new? What activities bring the best outcomes? Is your enthusiasm more than enough to get your child to try something new? Or what activities do you perform to convince and persuade him or her before he or she will test it out? Will he or she do anything his or her old sibling or cousin will?

- What's your teaching design and strategy? Do you describe verbally before you display? Do you present it step-by-step with commentary? Do you perform by gently demonstrating? Do you set items up and allow your child to find out what's happening by himself?

- How much time have you got to potty train your child? Are you available all day together with your kid or home only at a specific time of the day? Will you devote an uninterrupted chunk of the period to get started, accompanied by snippets of time each day afterward? Or are you considering fitting training into your already busy schedule?

- What are your targets? What do you consider would be much easier for you: changing diapers or assisting your son or daughter on the potty? Would you instead concentrate intently on potty schooling for two weeks and move issues along? Or do you read articles to teach and train while you let your son or daughter set the speed, mastering one stage at a time?

- Who'll be the teachers? Do you want to potty train by yourself? Or will several people be involved in the training?

Most of these issues can affect the toilet/potty training experience. Taking time to examine these points can help you plan the best strategy for you, your son or daughter, and the others of your loved ones, too.

Factors that Enhances Effective Training

Whether you are employing elimination communication with a three-month-old, pre-training an eighteen-month-old, or introducing a brand-new concept to a three-year-old, there are two important factors that may affect the process above all, both of these factors will establish the pace for potty training. These could make the toilet schooling journey a demanding, unpleasant event, or even ensure that it is an excellent, successful process.

These two factors could make your son or daughter miserable or make him or her content. They can make any strategy an unexpected disaster, or they can make nearly every potty/toilet training method work beautifully.

What exactly are these excellent factors? ***The teacher's attitude and the teacher's degree of patience.***

Allow me to say this again to ensure that you grasp this essential concept. *Both factors which will set the speed for potty training effectiveness are your **attitude as well as your patience***.

You'll remember that I didn't mention anything about the mentee or student! That's because kids learn factors from their parents and other folks in their life, which is what they practice. And kids are like small sponges. Children are continually watching others, specifically the adults in their life. They grab cues from others about how exactly they should respond in a variety of situations; whether it's the first time on an equine, the first flavor of papaya or the first take a seat on a potty chair, your child will end up being learning from you.

So, no matter where your son or daughter is in the readiness department, and regardless of what approach you choose to take, be sure that these factors are in proper place before starting potty training process.

The two important indicators for effective and successful toilet schooling process popularly known as potty training are;

i. The teacher's positive and supportive attitude.

ii. The teacher's kind and understanding tolerance.

CHAPTER 6

Sure-Fire Potty Training Strategies

Once you've decided about how you'll approach potty training with your kid and gathered all of your supplies, it's nearly time to start the process actively. Following are a few points to consider as you progress.

Keep in mind the two miracle factors; the teacher's excellent attitude and kind patience will set the pace for the toilet or potty-training journey. Take a breath, relax, and appreciate the knowledge with your baby.

Take It Slowly

If you feel relaxed about the procedure, it's likely your son or daughter will as well. Ironically, the much less you push, the quicker the outcomes will occur.

The more you hurry, the much longer it will require. Even if a day time or an additional deadline looms, don't hurry the process with an excessive amount of strength and pressure. Being even more relaxed can help your child find out more conveniently and will get this to be less demanding for you too.

Dress Him or Her for Training Success

It's more challenging for a toddler to get to the toilet in time but having the complication of snaps, zippers, and buttons. Many a trainee managed to get to the toilet and then have a major accident standing before the toilet, wanting to undress. For another couple of months and probably actually longer, your son or daughter should, whenever possible, avoid wearing pants with buttons, snaps, belts, or zippers and T-shirts that hang beneath the waist. Be sure that your son or daughter can remove her clothes easily and quickly. Regarding dresses, get them short more than enough to be able to remove them completely and well taken care of.

The very best clothing for a fresh potty trainee is a T-shirt and shorts or slacks with an elastic waistband. Make certain these are relatively loose fit so that your son or daughter can easily have them up and down.

At the start of training, you might want to have your son or daughter actually remove his or her trousers and underwear when he or she uses the potty, because there are a great number of new things to consider and having a wad of jeans around his or her ankles could be distracting and partially lowered slacks can become splattered. If you do not have him remove his trousers, feel absolve to help him consider his clothing off and place them back on, also if he can perform it himself. Needing to dress and undress in about ten situations a day will work fast for a dynamic toddler and may result in disinterest in using the potty at all. Don't worry, though he or she will adapt to this section of the process very quickly.

Training Pants or Disposables (Diapers)?

Once your child gets a general idea and has started having daily success on the potty, you might want to change from diapers or disposable pull-up to cloth teaching pants to make things go along even faster.

The drawback to thickly padded disposable diapers or super-absorbent training pants is that they disguise wetness so very much that your son or daughter probably isn't bothered about it, whereas cotton training pants, or disposables with a stay-wet liner, signal wetness immediately and aren't extremely comfortable to wear when wet or messy. This can help your child to be more alert to what's happening down there.

Also, be sure you keep your son or daughter's pants a little loose so your baby can pull them easily. Training slacks or pull-ups ought to be a size larger than necessary. You desire them to be manageable for your son or daughter, without being so big that they droop.

Less Clothing Strategy

If you're fortunate to begin training in warm weather, or when you can turn heat up in your house during training, hold your toddler in only training pants for a week roughly. Children often resist coping with ON/OFF requirement during teaching, since it takes so very much time and effort based on their limited skills. Therefore, the less clothing to cope with, the better!

Some parents let their children roam naked during training, but it isn't for everyone. Consider it before you bring in the theory to your baby, because he or she is more likely to like the freedom and could surprise you by carrying out a bit more of it than you expect. You might want to consider your family's method of nudity. How are things managed during bath time? How can you respond if your son or daughter walks in when you are dressing? If your family culture is certainly one of modesty and you suddenly let your son or daughter roam the home naked, it could send him or her some complicated mixed messages.

However, some families are even more relaxed about your body's natural state. Kids, siblings, and parents bathe jointly, toddlers play in the toilet as Mommy showers and dresses, and little males potty trained while peeing alongside Daddy. If this describes your family style, then you might look for a small extra time to help your child tune in with her body's elimination process.

One of the various other things to take into account here is that whenever using the naked strategy, all those early mishaps (among several others) will be unhindered by clothes and property unprotected wherever your son or daughter might be, and it will not be his or her fault or whatever you can prevent. For those who have carpeting or home furniture that may be ruined by accidents, you may take working out of the backyard or choose to go the almost naked approach instead and pop a set of training jeans on your little one.

Make the Potty Child-Friendly

Can your child easily open the door and turn on the light? Reach the toilet paper? Get right up to the sink? If he or she is facing difficulty addressing and using her potty, she'll be less thinking about using it routinely. Also, if she counts on you to perform everything on her behalf, you'll be passing up on a wonderful facet of potty teaching: encouraging your son or daughter's independence is vital.

Many small children are suspicious of empty rooms, and several fear the dark. There is nothing scarier compared to the cavern of a dark toilet. Through the training months, and perhaps actually for an extended period after schooling, accept that you'll either need to accompany your kid each time or keep the way and toilet carefully well to chase apart any unwanted shadows.

Potty Training Abroad/Far from Home

New trainees could just be getting more comfortable with the potty routine in the home but are unlikely to really have the same success in public areas or while traveling from one place to another. It could be irritating for a mother or father to have to handle repeated incidents in the automobile or while abroad or away from home. There are numerous methods to handle being abroad with a kid in training.

You can simply opt to keep your son or daughter in diapers or disposable pants when abroad. Most children very easily adjust to the idea that there exists a change into diapers or pull-ups when you go out. Create a schedule: the kid goes potty and places on pull-ups before you go out and then adjusting back to training trousers or underwear when you come back home.

Other options listed below are to put your son or daughter's diaper or pull-ups more than his training jeans or make use of a waterproof diaper cover more than his training slacks. He may experience been happier if he will keep his big boy trousers on, yet he'll experience the wetness if he comes with an accident. It's sort of a mid-step that may keep you calm in the automobile while helping him discover that he or she is growing up.

If you'd prefer never to put your son or daughter on diapers when you are away your home, ensure that you are ready to handle on-the-street potty phone calls and potty mishaps. Bring along a portable potty for use in the automobile and a folding chair adapter for use in toilets. Cover the automobile seat with plastic material, and for cleanup, provide along wet wipes, plastic material luggage, and paper towels. Prepare yourself with a complete change of clothing, and perhaps socks and shoes.

And be sure you bring your persistence and good humor, as well. You will have bad incidents, therefore accept them, clean them up, change your son or daughter's clothes, and move on.

Naps and Bedtime

Many children will remain in nighttime diapers for a year or much longer after daytime achievement. Nighttime dryness is attained only once a child's biology facilitates this, you can't hurry it, so don't also try. (Occasional bed-wetting is known as normal until approaching age six.)

Maintain a routine of placing diapers or disposable pull-up on your kid for naps or bedtime. The moment he or she is awake, remove it and also have him or her utilize the potty because so many children will eliminate soon after getting up. Switch your son or daughter out of night time diapers when the morning hours diaper is regularly dry.

Have a Realistic Expectations

Understanding how to master toileting is normally a huge task for just a little child (kids). Mastery comes into play with time and patience. Sometimes will be more effective in some children than others. Sometimes when the house is tranquil and the day to day routine is definitely in place, your son or daughter will significantly have more success.

CHAPTER 7

Potty training For Kids Younger than 20 Months, Over the Age of Three Years

I usually recommend starting toilet/potty training between 20 and 30 months after birth. In my own vast experience, that's where in fact the magical home window of opportunity lays. Obviously, many people want to potty teach before 20 months, while some parents for reasons unknown have waited until after thirty months.

If you're toilet training before or after my recommended time-schedule it's still doable, but there are certain considerations which you should be aware of.

Potty Training Under 20 Months Old Kids

It is really completely possible to toilet teach under a few twenty months. A couple of things that may appear to you are:

Inadequate Communication

Consider your son or daughter is constantly communicating with you. It's your decision to decipher your son or daughter most likely reaches the "point and scream" stage. While this is a wonderful way to communicate, it's not necessarily effective when potty training. A very important thing to do is to instruct your son or daughter the indication for pee; this is *Standard American Sign language* or it could be constructed. However, I would recommend a vocal cue because oftentimes you aren't looking right at your son or daughter. The term pee is simple enough. Some mothers have used other vocals or can acknowledge particular screams. One mother determined her little girl made a particular clicking sound. It became their sign for "gotta go." I'd not get worried about differentiating between pee and poop as considerably as words. It's heading to come quickly enough. Tugging down the slacks and Physically manipulating clothes you certainly want to begin working on your son or daughter having the ability to manipulate his own clothes at the earliest opportunity. Obviously, as of this age your son or daughter will naturally become more reliant on you than teenagers would be.

Prompting

Your child would require more of you more than a mature child would. You are going to be fast on those easy catches I've described several times. You need to keep to heart that you will be accountable for your child peeing more than the mother or father of the two-year-old would be. Your son or daughter are certain to get it and can eventually initiate it individually over time, however they will require more help.

A Little Potty Seat is Essential

It's quite essential to have just a little seat available. I often get some good version of these scenario: *"We don't enjoy the tiny potty chair. We choose he learn directly on the big toilet, since that's where he'll be heading."* That's alright, I understand, but my question is, *"Don't you want him to have the ability to continue his own?"*

Until your son or daughter can physically maneuver onto the best toilet safely, he would need to get your help. I think it's really worth the twenty dollars to get the tiny potty. Quickly enough, he'll proceed to the big toilet. But if he gets the notion to be on his own, we certainly want to make it designed for him to do so.

Remember that it is likely to be considered a much longer process for younger child and definitely not harder, but much longer. Improvement can be slower, and that's alright. Just don't expect it to be done in a week. I find that to be quite rare. Your ultimate goal should be improvement, not perfection. As long as the thing is him making constant improvement, it's all good.

Be really prepared to inform everyone to frick off

In the event that you know in your gut that your child has the capacity to do this and you are feeling ready, do it now.

But society will let you know that up-down, and side-wise that you will be crazy. I really do not think this is so. I congratulate you on your intuition! Fantastic. Rock and roll on, Mama, and don't look back again.

Remember that the target is to move along with the timeline from being clueless to "I peed, I'm peeing, I have to visit the toilet." Each little element may take a little of your time. It's all good as long as you feel improvement.

The kid under twenty weeks can "not be setting it up" for some time before it clicks. You can still potty teach a kid who is just a little clueless, but it will require longer, and it's really heading to be about you. In the event that you work beyond the home and don't have a ready care supplier, you should probably wait around.

You don't know very well what kind of potty trainer you are till you jump in and do it now. At this age group, if it's not heading according to plan you can always re-diaper, and it'll not hurt the procedure one bit.

There's a lot happening developmentally before twenty

months, as well as your child just might not have the skill set. In the event that you feel in a position to be there and help, that's amazing. I'm not seeking to scare you or be considered a big bummer, but I wish to be realistic with you.

Potty Training Kids over 30 Months

If your son or daughter has ended thirty weeks but under thirty-six weeks, you're at risk of a danger zone, but you aren't fully in it yet.

The thing you should be familiar with is the behavior stuff. The level of resistance that originates from a kid over 30 weeks isn't usually because of learning. It's usually because you say one thing and they're automatically going to state another. The old child needs a lot more personal privacy, so absorb that. In addition they need a lot more self-reliance. The "leave" fast is the best. That's when you remind them in an informal way, such as, "I could see you have to pee. There's your toilet." And physically and mentally leave.

The older child is also probably going to have poop troubles. Paying close focus on the "glaring limelight." These old kids are much more mounted on the security blanket of diapers. Personal privacy and self-reliance are your very best wager. As I've said, thirty to thirty-six months is not really a danger area... just type of a no-man's land of fuzziness. It's time to really do that now, with conviction and persistence.

Potty training for Over 36 Months

If you ask me, this is actually the risk zone. I understand many people are persuaded that three is the modern to potty teach. If you ask me, it's infinitely harder.

So again, ditch the guilt. You are what your circumstance is, and we can't change that. Okay? I'm imagining you were "waiting till she was ready," and today she's showing no signals to be ready. Or you will need to enter a preschool. Or something clicked in your mind to accomplish this now.

In any case, it's significantly time to place your big mama panties on and really understand how this is done.

Whenever a child is three or older, there's actually hardly any learning on how to achieve in regard to the toilet.

It's highly improbable that your son or daughter is brand-new to toilet training. Most kids as of this age group have simply rejected your tries, whether it is in a huge, violent tantrum kind of way or a continuous peeing-in-pants a quiet way.

The very best analogy I could make is, say a youngster

has discovered twenty letters of the alphabet. That's a good chunk of the alphabet, right? But kind of worthless with no other six words. Now, you can't just throw those words at a child and expect him to place them to be able. You have to begin at A and then go to B and put the letters in to the alphabet. I understand and you understand that he's got A and B, but without heading back over them, a child will have no frame of guide in regard to the other six words.

Ditto with whatever struggles you are experiencing with toilet training. I don't know very well what went bad, and I'm guessing you don't know very well what went wrong. So just start over.

The largest problems I see in kids over three are behavior issues. This is actually the psychological process where your child begins to split up from you. This age group is proclaimed by pressing against you and limit assessment.

It's good and normal, however when you add pee and poop to the course, you've established yourself up for the grand-daddy of most powerful struggles. As I'm sure you understand. I'm not stating that to rub your nasal area in it, it's just good to learn what you are against.

The ultimate way to end a power struggle is to forget about your end of the rope.

You give this (responsibility for the training) to them. You don't argue. You don't cajole. You don't beg or negotiate. So you never, ever let them smell your dread.

You start that first day with, "We've not done a good job with toilet training, so I'm heading to help you learn it the proper way. You're heading to help by allowing me know when you yourself have to pee or by heading yourself. There's the tiny toilet or the big toilet. You are able to choose." Most kids are actually waiting for you to arrive with the persistence. I'm not stating that's always the situation, but often it is. So here you are, looking forward to them, and all of this time, they've been waiting for you.

If, throughout that day, you are met with level of resistance, you keep up to cool off. For example, use that Get away prompt "You must pee, there is your toilet." You need to leave room for him to help make the good decision himself. This may take a day or two, so show patience. You intend to dance along the sensitive line between prompting and backing off.

Now, for some parents, that is heading to be adequate. Time upon time, I've seen mothers surprised at how efficiently it went with a former toilet strategy. Often , I must say I think it's a matter of uniformity and heading back and learning. If a youngster doesn't "get" all the the different parts of a process (like toilet training), they have a tendency to stop caring.

A whole lot of level of resistance in the old kid is basically because they haven't learned something the correct way.

CHAPTER 8

Advance Steps to Potty Training

In most cases it is recommended to start potty lessons with your son seated to pee. The principal reason for that is that if you train him to pee taking a stand, you'll be splitting toilet teaching into two separate stages: *urination and bowel schooling.*

Be Prepared to Access a Toilet Swiftly

Even before your son or daughter asks, ensure that you always know where exactly the toilet is; if you are in a shop, a friend's house, or anywhere else. In this manner, you can move quickly whenever your child announces the necessity to go pee or poo.

A child who is not used to these potty lessons might wait before last minute to announce his or her necessity to go pee or poo. Whenever your child says she's pressed, reach the potty and perform it quickly! While it's occasionally annoying to need to quit everything to consider taking him or her to the toilet, this is specifically everything you have been wishing to achieve. Your son or daughter is recognizing the desire and delaying elimination until he or she reaches the toilet. So show patience and support, even though the urgent quest may cause you to quit whatever you are doing at the moment.

Get Your Kids to learn potty Indicators

If your child is worked up about potty training and seems to be getting the hang of it, or in case you have a potty dead collection you need to meet, you might help speed up the procedure.

Select a day when you'll be home all day and will have

no outdoor engagement. Give your son or daughter lots of salty snack foods and juice or drinking water or beverage. Watch him or her cautiously for indicators to pee or poo, or set a timer or maintain a log to ensure that you keep in mind the approximate time to execute a potty function every 30 mins. Make an effort to think of methods to make this a great event.

The ideology is that; taking more liquid in means even more liquid out, so you should have lots of practice appointments to the toilet. And everybody knows that practice makes ideal perfection!

If your son or daughter spends time in someone else's care, make sure everyone communicates with one another relating to your child's potty teaching. Have a clear plan for potty training to ensure that everyone is constant whenever taking care of your child.

Exercise Patience during Accidents

Accidents are likely to happen during the training period. Utilize the same approach you utilize when she buttons her sweater the wrong manner or spills some milk. *"Oops. Missed the potty at that point. Don't worry, pretty soon you'll get it right."*

Accidents are extremely normal, especially in the beginning of training. Nevertheless, if your son or daughter is having a lot more accidents than successes, or if either you or your son or daughter is getting distressed about these incidents, you might want to retake the readiness quiz to observe only if you've started a little too early.

Accidents are inevitable initially, however they should steadily decrease. If indeed they continue after your son or daughter has completed training, nevertheless, you might need to examine the reason for them. If your son or daughter is just too busy to avoid her activity to access the toilet, perhaps you're in best position to make it possible for him or her to recuperate from these episodes. You might like to get her more mixed up in cleanup process. Train your child how precisely to help clean up any mess, change his or her personal clothing, and put her filthy pants in the laundry. If she's to help you look after all of this, it could help reduce these mishaps. It's typical for a kid to master taking care of potty schooling before another, so avoid being surprised of accidents happening for some time. Just maintain praising her successful attempts and keep focusing on the less-consistent process.

Offer Incentive to Encourage Potty Learning

In case you are not certain that your son or daughter is physically ready for potty training, I'd advise against using any type of prize system. If he or she is physically unable to utilize the potty individually, you'll just be establishing him or her up for disappointment.

If, however, your child is set physically for potty schooling but is reluctant emotionally or adapting to the theory slowly, you might help spark the process with reward or "potty prizes." Regardless of what you've considered giving kids prizes as rewards previously, there are occasions to utilize this effective idea during potty teaching. According to some polls, a lot more than 80 percent of parents conforms to giving their children benefits or prizes for using the potty, so you would be in good company.

Survey has revealed that most kids and preschoolers could be highly motivated to create adjustments when offered prizes-which, I'm sure, is a great surprise for you! There are many approaches you may use.

Be Calm and Patient

This whole process does take time. You almost certainly won't feel confident to completely start your son or daughter's toileting for most months. So relax, show patience, and revel in the journey. Kids are just little for an extremely short time to embrace the training effectively.

Offer Encouragement to your Kid

Some specialists say that you need to give a whole load of positive opinions, including a partylike atmosphere-actually with noisemakers, cake, and party hats. Others state that you ough to avoid getting overly thrilled or emotional and acknowledge that your son or daughter has done well.

The proper answer is that the proper answer is different for each parent and child pair. Some parents are naturally more thinking about everything their kids perform; others tend to be reserved.

Some women thrive on the parents' energy, other kids are easily overwhelmed. Even two different kids in the same family will respond easily to different degrees of enthusiasm.

Probably the finest advice is to accomplish what comes naturally. What's most significant is that you would like your child to learn that you support him, that you will be pleased with his efforts and also his successes.

Chapter 9

Never Take Hand Cleaning with Levity

Cleaning hands after using the toilet is usually a major deterrent to the pass on of germs and contamination, yet research demonstrates many adults don't routinely clean their hands after toilet appointments, and several don't do a sufficient job of washing if in any case they carry it out. While 95% of women and men surveyed say they clean their hands after utilizing a public restroom, about 50% actually do it, based on the outcomes of an observational research.

Women surveyed were considerably more likely than males to state that they clean their hands.

"Hand washing may be the simplest, most reliable thing people may do to lessen the spread of infectious diseases," according to Julie Gerberding, M.D., director of a

healthcare facility Infections System, Centers for Disease Control and Avoidance.

You can instill this healthy lifelong hand-washing habit in your son or daughter by building a standard section of the potty check out every time, whether he makes a deposit or not. Most children like to perform and splash water, so with just a little encouragement, your son or daughter will happily adopt this concept.

Just make sure to have a durable step stool to ensure that your child can simply reach the sink. Select colourful soaps, foam soap dispensers, or child-friendly soaps. You may even ensure to have several variations available to ensure that he or she makes a choice about which to make use of. Don't hurry the process, and make certain he or she lathers up, which may be great fun. Supervise an intensive rinsing, and also have an easy to get towel for drying off.

You can motivate your kid's independence by teaching him or her how specifically to do this alone.

CHAPTER 10

Solution to Common Toilet Training Problems

If you have been thoughtful, patient and organized, toilet training might not go according to strategy. There are plenty of typical complications that appear during the schooling process. The most typical problems are teaching resistance, excessive incidents, refusal to have a bowel motion on the potty, constipation etc. The very best spot to start is usually to contemplate the many usual known reasons for toilet teaching complications and find if you cannot figure out the reason for the issue. This chapter provides specific suggestions and solutions for the issues that these circumstances cause through the potty training process.

The first rung on the ladder to solving any issue is to

have a deep breath and do it again after me (using the power of confessions): *"My kid will figure out how to make use of the toilet. They all do. This as well shall move."* More than 98 percent of children grasp daytime toileting by age four, and with persistence and the proper plan of actions, your child are certain to get there, too.

The Most Commonly Known Reasons for Toilet Training Problems

- The child isn't ready (lacks the correct physical skills).

- The child isn't ready (emotionally, socially, or behaviorally).

- The child doesn't know very well what he or she's supposed to do (communication).

- The child is becoming too distracted with something else to value going potty.

- The kid is uninterested in training.

- The child can be fearful of, or unpleasant with, some aspect of training.

- Existence of a power struggle between your child and the parent.

- There's too much tension and pressure surrounding the process.

- The mother or father has unrealistic expectations.

- The parent isn't carrying out a toilet training program; it's hit or miss.

- The parent isn't ready (lacks time, endurance, or desire to carry out an idea).

- The mother or father and caregiver don't acknowledge an idea and are sending mixed messages.

- The mother or father is confusing normal mishaps with failure.

- The routine doesn't match the child's elimination pattern.

- The strategy used doesn't match the child's learning style or personality.

- The strategy used doesn't fit the parent's personality or teaching design.

- There exists a physical or medical deterrent (such as constipation, disease, or uncontrolled allergies).

Another important idea to understand is that you could lead a kid to the potty, nevertheless, you can't help to make him or her fill it. That is your child's undertaking, not really yours. You can teach her, you can prepare the required tools, and you will maintain positivity and supportive, but maybe for the very first time in her youthful life, the greatest result is completely in her power.

Potty training appears like a huge little bit of chocolate cake. With a part of ice cream. Sprinkled with chocolates! Maybe even more amazing.

Endeavor to examine the prior list of commonly known reasons for toilet teaching problems and make an effort to figure out which part of it are obtainable in the form of effective toileting mastery for your son or daughter. After you have a deal with one of those fundamental reasons, it'll open up your brain to all types of new solutions. Afterward, read over the topics that adhere to that match your problems.

Potty Training Resistance

You thought your son or daughter was ready. You believed you were ready. But things aren't going according to strategy. Following are some typically common mother or father statements with challenges and solutions.

"He Won't Even Try!"

If your child appears totally clueless, he probably is. For his lifetime he's peed and pooped in his diaper rather than also noticed this elimination. Right now you want him never to only notice but keep it and then place it some-where else! It is time to go through potty books, have a sibling, friend, or parent demonstrate; provide a few step-by-step lessons; and maybe have even some bare naked playtime to greatly help him observe and experience what's happening straight down there.

It's possible that your son or daughter offers to try but feels more overwhelmed. He might have had high anticipations for himself and feels he's failed. He might just need help knowing that this is not a one-day work but will need him quite a long time to learn. Compliment him for the things he can do, regardless of how little, and build on those.

I'd also recommend that you retake the readiness quiz by accessing several readiness quiz freely available online and ponder on each issue, rather than tagging down the solution that you desire to be right, indicate what's actually true. Your son or daughter might not be prepared just yet. And in the event that you currently know that, but nonetheless you need to continue potty schooling, refill your basket of tolerance, place a smile on your own face, and grab the fanciest methods in this book.

"She's tantrums when I make her take a seat on the potty."

If your son or daughter views sitting down on the toilet as a punishment, it's likely there's been an excessive amount of stress or pressure on her. If things are actually awful, you may need to stop teaching for a week or two to provide you both a breather. However, for those who have made some progress, you might not want to stop what you've achieved. Rather, make potty period more pleasurable. Add books, play toys, music, storytelling, or singing to your toilet training strategy. Begin the fun before she actually sits straight down by having a parade of elimination into the toilet. Virtually all kids thrive with a parent's lighthearted one-on-one playtime, so concentrate on this aspect for some time, without challenging a deposit each time she uses the potty.

When you are feeling your baby is enjoying potty visits,

then start to take her in a regular schedule of each one and half to two hours or whenever she appears like she must go. When she starts to be successful, then compliment her and offer her with a sticker or prize. Quickly she'll dominate and end up being independent.

"I've tried everything in the book."

What may be the issue! Your poor small pottier is indeed confused he doesn't understand which end is certainly up! Have a step back and refine your program. Don't allow it to get complicated. Go over the potty-training guidelines to assist you clarify your potty schooling plan to ensure that it really is simple and clear.

Excessive Accidents

It's common for kids to have accidents if they are not accustomed to using the potty bowl. But if incidents don't gradually fade out as time passes, or if your son or daughter is having more experience moving in her slacks down in her potty, it may seem training is certainly going nowhere. Following certainly below are a few comments and recommendations.

"He comes with an accident each day!"

If your son or daughter is not used to potty training, it really is flawlessly normal for him to have a number of accidents each and every moment of commencement of training. Even kids who've been trained for half a year or even more may have a major accident once a week. The very best solution is usually to be ready for these with appropriate cleaning materials, quick access to a change of clothing, and a calm attitude.

One approach that will help reduce the amount of accidents is that you should become familiar with your son or daughter's signals of impending desire to visit the toilet and take your son or daughter to the potty when you suspect he or she must go. Do not request if he must go, because he'll most likely say no. Rather, invite him to check out by saying, *"Let's go potty."* Or provide a choice, saying, *"Do you wish to make use of your potty or the big toilet?"* Or just hold him by the hands and lead him to the toilet, saying, *"Come with me, kiddo."*

There's one very last thing to consider.

Do you provide your son or daughter more attention (great or poor) when he comes with an incident than when he provides achievement?

Turn the tables. Tidy up mishaps quickly and without

emotion, and offer lots of compliment, hugs, and interest for each productive potty visit.

"She never helps it be released into the toilet. It usually goes into her pants."

Your child might not be hearing her body when it tells her it is time to go. Or she gets so occupied with her play that she attempts to yank it apart, or she thinks she can take it a lot longer than she can really.

You may consider moving the potty nearer to her and which makes it easier on her behalf to go. Create a potty nook near her play region and maintain her dressed in very easy clothes. Once she gets utilized to heading when she must, you can move the potty seat back again to the toilet.

You may try having a potty party weekend. Don't

announce this to your child, just make an idea in your own brain. Stay house all weekend and go out in the same space as your baby. Provide plenty of salty snack foods and a lot to drink. Check her for signals and lead her to the potty once you think she might need to proceed, plus execute a potty operation every hour roughly. Give stickers, little prizes, or treats (think about her preferred salty chips?) to maintain her motivated and interested. The hidden benefit to this strategy is that you could like a weekend of one-on-one quality time together with your precious little kid.

Constipation and Refusal to have a Bowel Movement on the Potty

One of the most common and frustrating toilet training roadblocks is whenever a kid is unwilling to pee on the potty but needs a diaper, or uses his slacks, for bowel motions. Some children will in actuality hold their bowel motions and create serious constipation, which additional complicates the issue.

Children typically resist bowl movement on the toilet, or restrain from going, for just one of these reasons:

- Bowel motions take too long to hold back, and a dynamic child dislikes needing to take a seat on the potty for a protracted length of time.

- After being accustomed to the squashed feeling of stool coming out right into a diaper, the sensation of allowing it to loose in to the air is normally unsettling and strange.

- A child is accustomed to standing or shifting during a bowel motion and sitting even on the potty can be an uncomfortable change of schedule.

- Your son or daughter thinks the stool is usually part of his being and doesn't realize why he ought to flush it away.

- A poor experience, such as ending up being splashed on the bottom level with urine or water during elimination or having a messy incident, causes a child to avoid having it happen again.

- Discomfort from a previously hard or hard stool makes a kid afraid to poop on the potty.

- A current case of constipation which is stopping usual elimination.

Don't try to resolve the problem without understanding why it exists. Once you determine your son or daughter's impetus for staying away from bowel motions, you can generate the perfect strategy to help him or her have a natural elimination process.

CHAPTER 11

Do's and Don'ts of Potty Training

What to Do During Potty Training

- Make certain that your son or daughter is drinking a lot of water the whole day. Stick to drinking water and juice (apple, pear, cranberry, grape, and prune juice however, not orange or various other citrus juices).

- Be sure your son or daughter eats lots of fiber-rich foods each day: vegetables (especially natural ones), fruit, wholegrains, brownish rice, and oatmeal are a few examples. Avoid giving your son or daughter junk food, refined sugar, soda, candy, and chocolate.

- Limit foods that may constipate, such as bananas,

rice, apple-sauce, cheese, citrus juice, and carbonated sodas.

- Meals allergies or lactose intolerance (intolerance to milk products) could cause constipation in a kid. If you suspect this could be true, speak to your doctor.

- If your child shows been constipated, apply petroleum jelly or diaper ointment to her anus before potty appointments.

- Ensure that your child has lots of daily exercise, which stimulates digestion, prevents constipation, and is essential for proper elimination.

- End up being sure that your son or daughter is peeing every hour and two hours. Regular urination can be a necessary element to regular bowel motions.

- Take your son or daughter to the potty first thing in the morning and 10 to 30 mins after a complete meal, when BMs (bowel motion) will probably happen.

- Teach your son or daughter to move when the desire hits. Explain that the poop is wanting to come out and she would need to go to the toilet.

- Purchase a soft, cushioned child's adapter seat for the toilet or a potty chair with a soft seat. Some children find it hard to take a seat on the hard surface area for the amount of time it requires to have a bowel movement.

- If you discover your child has experienced a bowel movement in her slacks, calmly take her to the toilet. Flush her poop straight down the toilet with a comment to clarify that is where it goes. Also get her take a seat on the potty while you wipe her buttocks and let her understand that soon she'll perform her poop on the potty herself.

- If your child is only going to proceed in a diaper, start to have her do thus in the toilet. Progress to making her take a seat on the potty, in her diaper if she'd like. Once she can be used to this, recommend making her diaper off and placing it in to the potty bowl as a "pocket" to capture her poopie.

- You will probably find success by slicing through the crotch of the diaper to ensure that it is still wrapped around her, however the bottom is available to allow poop drop into the potty.

- Help to make sure that your son or daughter sits long enough to empty her bladder or bowel every time she uses the toilet. Make it a soothing 3 to 5 minutes.

- Make certain that your son or daughter's legs are comfortable, with knees slightly aside and foot firmly planted on the floor or a durable stool.

- Help your child unwind on the potty by reading books, telling a tale, singing a song or listening to one, or chatting.

- Have your son or daughter close her eye and have a few deep breaths while you chat or sing softly.

- Play soothing music during potty sits.

- If your child is showing signs of needing to poop but isn't having the achievement in the toilet, try having him lean ahead and rest his chest muscles against you when you gently rub his lower back. You can also get him sit backward on the toilet and lean against the container.

- Go through books about using the potty, especially those that discuss poop.

What You Never Should Do During Potty Training

- Do not get angry. Don't scold your son or daughter or make him or her experience guilt or shame. Your baby isn't doing this deliberately, she isn't attempting to make you mad, and she doesn't know how to resolve this as much as you do.

- Don't make your son or daughter take a seat on the toilet and "try" or push. BMs (bowel motion) happens when your body is prepared and forcing them can make little tears in the anus (fissures) or hemorrhoids, which cause all day discomfort in the rectum. This may cause the child to avoid pooping also may lead to constipation, which creates hard stool, which in turn causes even more hemorrhoids, and on to generate a dreadful routine of discomfort and frustration.

- Don't let your son or daughter stress when he sits to poo. Obviously, a small amount of pushing may be essential for a normal bowel motion. But if he's grunting, straining, and forcing, it's an indicator that either he's probably not set or he's relatively constipated. Have him drink a large glass of drinking water, eat a piece of fruit, and try again in ten or twenty minutes later.

- Don't ever help to make your son or daughter "hold it." When she announces the necessity to go, or if you observe that her body indicators are indicating to go, look for a toilet immediately. Delaying and keeping plays a part in constipation and additional bowel problems.

CHAPTER 12

Causes of Setbacks & Regressing during Potty Training

About 80 percent of parent's report suffering toilet training setbacks, therefore you are in extremely good business! There are over a million factors that contribute to kids who are experiencing great achievement with toilet training suddenly move totally backward. Here are some of the more commonly known reasons for setbacks:

- There exists a change in the family members or a disruption in the house, such as relocation, a fresh baby, divorce, marriage, houseguests, or the holiday season.

- The child is uninterested in the toilet training regimen.

- A sickness or damage of the kid or parent

interferes with the most common daily routine for times or weeks.

- There's been a drastic modification in routine, such as starting day treatment, a sibling heading off to college, or an at-home mother or father going off to function.

- The kid has mastered toilet teaching but then has numerous accidents that erode self-confidence. Perhaps an especially embarrassing general public episode takes place, or the unthinking feedback of a member of family or stranger yielding your child experience inadequacy with potty exercise. She may have decided it might be safer if she returned to diapers.

- Your child might have been successful at potty training since you were very successful in reminding him or her to proceed at the proper times. Over time of success you halted reminding him, therefore accidents started to occur.

Setbacks are always temporary; normally, we'd discover second graders putting on diapers. So, whenever a setback occurs with your child, simply set yourself back, right with your kid, and repeat the activities that were effective for you in the past. For instance, if her potty poster was popular, make a fresh one.

Tuck aside your own injured satisfaction, because this has nothing in connection with your task as an instructor nor will it mean your son or daughter has failed potty training. It simply means your son or daughter is normal. Show patience, be supportive, and quickly your baby will be back again to potty success.

When to Contact a Doctor

You should contact your wellbeing provider anytime you have concerns on the subject of your child's health. Listed below are a few of the signs that could warrant a telephone call to a doctor:

- Your child hasn't got a bowel motion in four or more days.

- There is bleeding in your child's urine or stool.

- Your child has a fever, is normally nauseous, or is vomiting.

- Your son or daughter isn't urinating every several hours.

- Your son or daughter has problems starting a blast of urine, even when he or she's to pee.

- Your child's urine has a foul smell.

- Your child's belly is protruded, hard, or swollen.

- Your son or daughter's underwear is generally smeared with stool, and it's unrelated to poor wiping practices.

- Your son or daughter is potty qualified but suddenly regresses for no apparent cause.

- You're getting excessively angry over the situation.

Toilet training complications can be quite frustrating and so are one of the significant reasons of child misuse. If you are finding this a great deal to handle, call a reliable friend or a healthcare professional.

If your son or daughter is having difficulty using the toilet, or if toilet training has turned into a main issue in your household, your physician will help you. He or she may analyze the improvement of toilet training, give you advice about diet adjustments, or put your son or daughter on a dietary fiber supplement, stool softener, or moderate laxative, if necessary.

Any child, regardless of how healthy, wise, or able, can have toilet training problems. Any mother or father, no matter how smart or experienced, would want help solving these complications. You shouldn't be shy or embarrassed about seeing a specialist on issues with toilet training. This common, and experts talk to parents each day on this topic.

CHAPTER 13

Potty Training and Habit

Firstly, I have to cover some ground on the subject of boundaries and limits; after that, I'll hit particular behaviors I've seen in potty schooling. Boundaries and limitations have a poor rap in parenting lately. They can appear mean or draconian or too authoritarian. Many parents don't have confidence in any consequence or discipline. I want to state outright: *I do not advocate, nor do I believe in hitting or beating a kid ever.*

This is most likely the trickiest issue addressed in this book separating out behavioral conduct from potty training. There exists a lot for your son or daughter to understand when potty teaching your children. Certainly, the first couple of days, and maybe actually the first couple of weeks, are filled with learning. Learning, naturally, requires making some errors and/or having some incidents. However, there exists a difference between learning and behavior or habit. When your kid is showing behavior, and after all of the poor variety, the behavior must be addressed.

You are potty training around two-year age range, and around the same time, you might see various other two-year-old behavior. This might well be the first time you are seeing your child act, but it's normal. The awful twos aren't only a cliché; they are real. Throughout normal development, your son or daughter must test limitations. It's his work. He needs to find out where the fence is, as they say. The reason your wall in your backyard is there is indeed not to make your child wander and get misplaced. Limits and boundaries will be the fence in your child's psyche. With them intact, just while in your backyard, your child feels safe and sound, knowing where he may go and may not go.

A trend in contemporary parenting is to assume that the kid is with the capacity of deciding good stuff for himself without having to be provided any boundaries or limits. That is not the case. I frequently look to the Montessori system for how exactly to allow children to make some decisions while also providing boundaries. Within a framework, the kids are absolved from making choices; however they are not free to carry out whatever it is they need.

The children all consume lunch collectively. You can't make a couple of kids get a snack in the fridge and leave this up to them to choose if they are hungry, it could lead to mayhem. The kids all go outside jointly, whether one is tired or not really. Our children need some fences. Within those fences, we can enable tremendous freedom.

What I see, both from my experience and in my work is that most of us parents have a problem with providing freedom within boundaries. In our quest to improve free-thinking, kids are not offered enough framework to allow them to feel safe.

I see kids raised with no limitations or boundaries who by enough time they are age five or six, are wild and incredibly hard to control. By this, after exhibiting out-of-control behavior, not that they must be "controllable" just like a puppet.

Imagine the stress your child would feel if you were driving, been at the backseat, and he or she has zero idea of where you were heading. I've extrapolated that idea even more. Imagine if your son or daughter were responsible for providing you the directions, and which you followed their instructions. Proceed left. Go right. No. Stop. Wow. You'd quickly be lost, yes? That's where points will get mucky with the oft-touted child-led style of parenting. You could be child-led for the reason that you pay attention to and validate your son or daughter's opinion, but you just can't follow your child's lead through life. Both of you will get dropped. *The automobile you are driving is usually life, and it's your task to learn where you are going.* Ironically, most of the parents I've known in my own personal life are striving to give the youngster a "freedom" childhood. Still, how free is your son or daughter if he's entirely responsible for the direction the automobile is traveling. It's hugely anxiety-provoking. A free childhood ought to be about chocolate or vanilla, and something else.

All this is especially true in case you have a spirited or strong-willed child. I frequently work with parents who have a kid fitting this explanation. This child is generally demanding and will be challenging with regards to potty training as well. Still, this child requires boundaries and limits just as much as, or even more than, your garden-variety child.

All well and great, but what does this need to do with potty training?

Well, occasionally behavior kicks up during potty teaching. And because potty schooling is so wrought with emotion, it becomes hard to draw it aside from behavior. I also discover that parents will endure all types of behavior during potty schooling that they wouldn't work in other circumstances.

For example, one of the primary challenges parents today encounter during potty training gets their child to take a seat on the potty. Yes, you can go through to them or sing to them. I state it's alright to play with a mobile device seeing that as a distraction in the beginning. But, when you inquire your son or daughter to sit to go potty, your son or daughter should sit. Today, to a lot of individuals that sounds severe.

You show your son or daughter to sit and they don't. *How can you handle that?*

I'm requesting because-whatever your response is, that's how you're likely to handle it during potty training. When it's supper, it's time to sit and consume. When it's potty period, it's time to take a seat on the potty.

Once you encounter behavior during potty training, do your very best to put it right into a different context. That will assist you to figure out how better to deal with it in the context of potty schooling. It's your parenting duty. I do not really nor have I ever comfy telling people the way to handle behavior generally. That's why I'm providing you a framework to work with, and you may make your own parenting decisions.

Many parents say, "We don't feel safe making him sit." I agree. I don't believe you should force your son or daughter to sit. Nevertheless, it's worth pondering precisely how fearful we are because of the potty. Many parents dread doing anything unfavorable around potty training. Utilizing a firm or stern voice seems contrary to these parents, and they're worried about traumatizing the kid. This is where another scenario will come in handy. Everyone has held their kid down and strapped them in the car seat. Even though they are kicking, screaming, and hitting. We perform it because we should go somewhere, and we need them to be safe. Has your son or daughter ever been traumatized by that rather than wished to sit in the automobile front seat someday? I'm guessing No. Again, I'm not saying you should exert pressure on your child onto the potty or strap him down, or anything remotely like this. I'm simply pointing out that fear of traumatizing a kid by conveying the message that you mean business has gotten a bit out of control.

Another thing to bear in mind may be the difference between *"the kid you have" and "the kid you want."* You have a child you have, definitely not the kid you need. This is also true during potty training.

I can give you recommendations about any special conditions you might have, but we can not change your zebra's stripes. Still, that is hard for all of us to admit and hard to keep in mind. Most of us want the well-behaved,

loving, courteous kid. We got what we want. Still, our choice is fierce. When you are potty training, take care not to linger in the property of "I want him . . ." We can deal with what we have, but we can not cope with fantasy.

There's another aspect to "a child you have." If your son or daughter shows a particular "problem"- say he's whiny, or she's resistant or susceptible to histrionics and tantrums, you will have this same kid if you are potty teaching. No judgment; there is absolutely no behavior I've not really seen. Still, I discover parents who in some way think potty training will happen in a bubble-that the rest of the behavior the kid exhibits is somehow not likely to appear even though it's potty training. That is a big transition, so these behaviors can not only be right there, but they may get magnified for a brief period. Again, it's all great. Just keep your anticipations level as well as your love big.

Whatever your child's personality is, I can't change that or correct it; that's built-in the child's physiology. If your son or daughter is exhibiting the behavior you do not like, or you are feeling is usually disrespectful, you will likely see that same behavior during potty schooling. What I could tell you is how exactly to deal with a few of the behaviors you find in potty training.

Here's a clear exemplary case of behavior. Say your son or daughter did ideal for a couple of days. Suddenly, she doesn't want to utilize the potty anymore. This may appear to be a defiant "NO!" or it could seem she just can't be bothered with this. If she sat and peed/pooped on the potty several time, then we realize she can perform it, it's that easy. If she subsequently chooses never to, it's behavior.

In case you are feeling unfortunate or just a little heartbroken that it isn't heading as you intended, it's likely that your son or daughter needs more learning. If you feel as if you are being pranked, if you feel anger, or if you feel like strangling your kid, I'll wager it's behavior. Usually, parents have a pervasive sense when they are coping with behavior but don't carry out anything because they're terrified of "traumatizing" the kid.

Having boundaries and pursuing through won't traumatize your kid in any sense. When you have a youngster who you understand is taking part in you, the very best move to make is provide a small, instant, appropriate consequence. For example, take away the play toy he was using when he wet his slacks, or consider restraining him from the activity where he was involved.

Toddlers don't have that extended way of thinking. For this reason, sticker charts are ineffective. Toddlers don't have the thought process to state, "Wow. I've six stickers; yet another and I'll have a week of staying dry out!"

The small, immediate consequence can be helpful when you aren't sure whether he needs more learning or is exhibiting the behavior. I believe I've managed to get clear that satisfaction and self-mastery ought to be the motivation behind potty training a child effectively. However, for a few children that by no means clicks in, plus they need some exterior motivation to nudge things along. Some parents react such as, "But I'll feel terrible if I provide him a consequence, and he needs even more learning." Removing a little toy consequently won't scar your child forever. And it's the quickest way to get a remedy. If your child can't utilize the potty realizing that his toy is sure to get placed on the fridge for one hour if he doesn't, you can wager that so far he needs more to learn, and he won't be scared. If your child can do it all, you then know the incidents are because of behavior. I'm talking about real-world potty training, not theory. Effects are sure to get you your solution the fastest.

Some parents say, "Isn't a consequence only the opposite of an incentive? I'd rather give incentive for the behavior I want rather than provide a consequence for what We don't want." I am aware of the idea behind this and, yes, generally, positive reinforcement is most effective with children. Nevertheless, we get back to that notion of expected behavior. The problem with benefits and potty schooling is that they get sticky. The stakes must be continuously raised to ensure they work. If you are likely to reward for peeing, where else can that lead? I'd rather curb undesired behavior than prize the hell out of excellent behavior. Else, you finish up with a youngster who expects to end up being rewarded for everything.

I fully have confidence in benefits for exemplary behavior, and I also think that bad behavior gets a consequence.

Acknowledgments

Appreciation to God, friends and family. Most importantly all the readers of my book.

www.ingramcontent.com/pod-product-compliance
Lightning Source LLC
Chambersburg PA
CBHW061022220326
41597CB00017BB/2254